SOUNDBITES

Keyboards

Roger Thomas

Heinemann Library
Chicago, Illinois

Designed by Paul Davies and Associates
Originated by Ambassador Litho Ltd.
Printed at Wing King Tong in Hong Kong

06 05 04 03 02
10 9 8 7 6 5 4 3 2 1

Library of Congress Cataloging-in-Publication Data
Thomas, Roger, 1956-
  Keyboards / Roger Thomas.
      p. cm. -- (Soundbites)
Includes bibliographical references (p.   ) and index.
  ISBN 1-58810-263-7
  1. Keyboard instruments--Juvenile literature. [1. Keyboard
instruments.] I. Title. II. Series.
  ML549 .T46 2001
  786'.19--dc21

                              2001001723

Acknowledgments
The author and publishers are grateful to the following for permission to reproduce copyright material:
Cover photograph: Photodisc.
pp. 4, 6, 9, 11, 16, 18, 19, 21 Lebrecht Picture Library; pp. 5, 20 Jazz Index; pp. 10, 26 Redferns; p. 12
Eyewire; pp. 13, 14 Mary Evans Picture Library; p. 15 Corbis; pp. 17, 24, 29 Unknown; p. 22 Hulton; p.
23 Outline/Redferns; pp. 27, 28 Yamaha.

Special thanks to Brian Shea for his comments in the preparation of this book.

Every effort has been made to contact copyright holders of any material reproduced in this book.
Any omissions will be rectified in subsequent printings if notice is given to the publisher.

Some words are shown in bold, **like this.** You can find out what they
mean by looking in the glossary.

Contents

Introduction

Today, the instrumental keyboard is one of the first images that comes to mind when we think of music. The sequence of white keys overlaid with groups of two and three black keys is a strong visual reminder of how music seems to "work." The notes go from left to right, from the lowest to the highest—an entirely logical pattern, at least in **Western** music. The notes repeat in a regular pattern from one end of the keyboard to the other, with the difference between any two **adjacent** notes seemingly consistent. At any point on the keyboard, the distance between one note and another that falls in the same position of the repeated pattern, the **octave,** is constant.

A spread of notes

A left-to-right or low-to-high layout of notes is seen in many-stringed instruments, such as the **zither,** as well as in the tuned **percussion** instruments of many cultures, including Africa (the balafon), Java and Bali (gamelan instruments), and the West (orchestral tuned percussion). In combination with the development of mechanical keys, this concept led to the invention of the modern keyboard.

A left-to-right note layout is found on many different types of instrument in many cultures.

Origins

One theory proposes that the keyboard was the idea of an Italian Benedictine monk named Guido d'Arezzo (c. 990–1050), who also made important contributions to musical theory and **notation.** Another suggests that it was developed from the **hurdy-gurdy,** a stringed instrument that has buttons for holding the strings down at various points to change the notes. However, a keyboard is essentially a system of levers, and the idea of using this technique to control a musical instrument predates both d'Arezzo and the hurdy-gurdy.

The hydraulis

The hydraulis may have been the first true keyboard instrument. It was invented by an engineer named Ctesibius in the ancient city of Alexandria, Egypt in about 250 B.C.E. It was essentially a pipe organ, since the sound of the instrument came from flutelike tubes. Air was pushed into the instrument with hand pumps. However, Ctesibius devised a system that allowed a reserve air supply to build up inside the instrument. This system was regulated by water that flowed into the system to keep the air pressure constant even if the air was not pumped in with a constant rhythm. Early illustrations show that the hydraulis had either large keys, played with the palm of the hand, or **sliders** that were moved in order to let air into the pipes. This simple idea was used again in organ design centuries later.

This is a fourth-century drawing of a hydraulis.

Types of Keyboard Instruments

Today, keyboard instruments are commonly referred to as a group. As well as sharing the distinctive layout of keys that became the standard design by the middle of the fifteenth century, the basic method of playing all keyboard instruments is the same. However, the differences in how the various instruments respond when their keys are pressed means that many variations in technique—and lots of practice—are needed for a person to become proficient at playing multiple keyboard instruments.

The musicologists' method

An early system of classifying musical instruments was published in 1914 by two famous **musicologists** named Erich von Hornbostel and Curt Sachs. This system classifies instruments according to how they make sound: those with strings (**chordophones**); those that use wind (**aerophones**); those made of materials that naturally have a musical sound when struck, scraped, shaken, or rubbed (**idiophones**); drums and related instruments with membranes (**membranophones**); and mechanical and electrical instruments.

The interior of a piano clearly shows how it relies on mechanical design.

Keyboard groups

The keyboard family can be divided into groups based on how each instrument makes its sound. Here are five major groups and examples of instruments in each group:

- Instruments that use strings include the piano, that makes sound using a system of strings that are struck by felt-covered **hammers;** the harpsichord family, with strings that are plucked by a mechanical system; and the clavichord family, with strings that are struck by light metal hammers.

- The wind group includes the pipe organ and the reed organ or harmonium. These work by having air blown through pipes or across metal **reeds.**

- Idiophonic keyboard instruments include the celeste, with its keyboard-controlled hammers that strike metal bars. The original type of electric piano is similar, except that the sound comes from thin metal tongues, with the sound being **amplified** via **pickups** in the same way as with the electric guitar.

- Electromechanical instruments include the type of electric piano described above, as well as the **Clavinet** and the original type of electric organ (it produces sounds using motorized metal disks that spin in **magnetic** fields to produce electronic **tones**). This category also includes the Mellotron, an electric keyboard instrument that plays back a sound prerecorded on a length of tape every time a key is pressed.

- Electronic instruments can be distinguished from all other keyboard instruments in that they contain no moving parts other than the keys themselves. Each key simply acts as a switch to activate an electronic circuit.

How Keyboards Work

Although all keyboards have a similar layout (with the exception of a few experimental designs), the action that takes place when a key is pressed differs widely among the various types of instruments in this family. The only other thing all keyboard instruments have in common is that they all have some sort of casing that encloses the instrument. On **acoustic** instruments, such as the piano, this can contribute to the instrument's sound, as well as serving to protect its **components.**

A piano key

Each key on the piano activates a series of wooden levers that carry out a sequence of actions. First, a felt **hammer** is "flicked" so that it hits a set of strings, making them vibrate and producing a note. The hammer is immediately lifted off the strings, so that the full sound of the strings will be heard. At the same time, a **damper** that normally rests on the strings is lifted away. These dampers prevent the strings from vibrating when other notes are played. When the key is released, the hammer and damper return to their original positions, stopping the sound. A piano also has two or three pedals that affect the damper system to **sustain** notes longer or to give the instrument a "brighter" or "softer" **tone.**

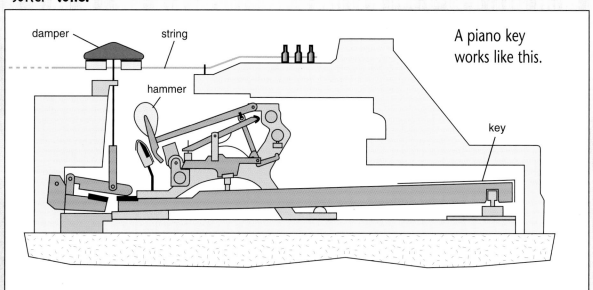

A piano key works like this.

damper · string · hammer · key

8

Harpsichords, clavichords, and organs

The harpsichord family not only includes the harpsichord but also encompasses the spinet and the virginal, two smaller instruments that work in a similar way. On these instruments, each key causes a small piece of bone to pluck the strings, in the same way a **pick** can be used to pluck the strings of a guitar.

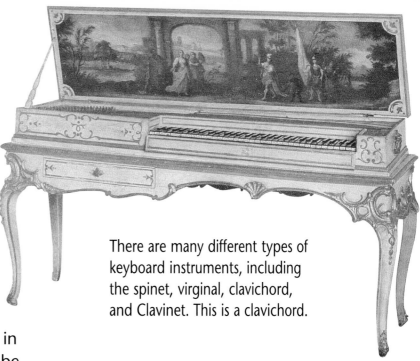

There are many different types of keyboard instruments, including the spinet, virginal, clavichord, and Clavinet. This is a clavichord.

On a clavichord, the keys cause thin metal hammers to strike metal strings inside the instrument.

The key mechanism on pipe and reed organs is attached to a device that pumps air through a system of **valves.** This process allows air to blow into flutelike pipes or across thin metal **reeds** to produce sounds.

Electromechanical and electronic instruments

This family includes the **Clavinet**—essentially a large **amplified** clavichord—and the original type of electric piano. In each case, the keys are mechanical, causing some form of hammer or striker to make contact with a small plate, bar, or tongue. The sound is then amplified electronically.

Sound-producing electronic circuits come in many designs, and different electronic keyboards may use one or several of these. However, in every case, the key mechanism is simply a switch that allows **electric currents** to pass into the instrument.

The Piano

The piano is one of the most widely recognized instruments in the world today, yet it is a comparatively recent invention. Around the middle of the eighteenth century, changing trends in pianos meant that more emphasis could be placed on the expressive power of music. Most keyboard music of that time was played on harpsichords. These used plucked strings to make sounds, but the instruments' **tone** was impossible to change, and harpsichords were unable to produce varied **dynamics.** Harpsichord makers tried to improve the instruments by using **shutters** and **dampers** and by adding a second keyboard that had extra strings or that plucked the strings in different places to give different tones. However, it was clear that a completely new instrument was needed.

Cristofori and Silbermann

The idea of the piano had actually begun during the previous century. Two instrument builders were largely responsible for the design of the piano as we now know it. The first was Bartolomeo Cristofori, who lived in Italy during the late seventeenth century. He devised an instrument, called the *arpicimbalo,* that was based on the dulcimer, a stringed instrument played by hand using **hammers.**

This square piano dates from 1817.

Cristofori first added a key mechanism to this instrument. Then he went on to build a group of instruments with soft mechanical hammers and keyboards. He called these *gravicembali col piano e forte,* or "harpsichords with soft and loud sounds." The strings were hit with hammers, and the loudness of the instrument could be changed by how hard it was played. This quality earned it the name *fortepiano* (a name still used for pianos of a very early design), as well as the more familiar *pianoforte* ("soft and loud")—the rarely used full name of today's piano. A German organ builder, Gottfried Silbermann (1683–1753), then improved on this design. By the early 1800s, composers such as Ludwig van Beethoven (1770–1827) began to use pianos that were soon to become similar to those used today.

Shapes and sizes

The piano became very popular, and instruments were made in many styles for use in different settings. Here are some examples of the different types:

The concert grand is the largest type of grand piano.

- The grand piano's winglike shape matches the slope of its soundboard and the lengths of the strings inside, from low-**pitched** (long and thick) to high-pitched (shorter and thinner). Some early instruments used this shape that remains the standard for performance pianos today. It is made in several sizes.

- The upright piano is designed in a space-saving vertical case. This makes it the most popular piano for use at home, in classrooms, or wherever space is limited. Early types of upright pianos kept the winglike shape of the grand piano, leading to designs known as the pyramid piano, the harp piano (with exposed strings like a harp), and even the giraffe piano.

- Historical pianos, such as the *fortepiano* and square piano, are still found today, as many pianists like to play on the exact instrument the composer was likely to have heard the composition on.

The Harpsichord Family

The harpsichord preceded the piano as the most widely used keyboard instrument for concert music. A great deal of the music that we think of today as piano music, such as the "Goldberg Variations" by Johann Sebastian Bach (1685–1750), were in fact originally written for the harpsichord and organ.

Early harpsichords were small and had thick, heavy cases. Later versions, like this one, however, had lighter casework and were highly decorative.

Early harpsichords

The first successful harpsichords were made in Italy in the 1500s, although instrument makers had already been experimenting with the basic principles of the instrument for two hundred years before that. The harpsichord can be made of various kinds of wood and has metal strings. Spinets and virginals are smaller instruments that work in basically the same way.

Later variations

The sound of the harpsichord is limited by its action. The notes cannot be **sustained**—as they can on a piano (by raising the **dampers**) or on a wind or **bowed** string instrument—because the plucking of a string produces only a short sound. Also, whenever a note is played, the mechanism must work with enough force to make the string "twang" cleanly, but this restricts the instrument's volume. This problem was noted by the eighteenth-century composer Couperin, who wrote in 1713 that he would be grateful to anyone who could "contrive to render this instrument capable of expression."

It was not until the invention of the piano that these problems were truly resolved. In the meantime, harpsichord builders worked hard to think of ways of improving their instruments. One idea was to add a second keyboard with more strings, with the mechanisms of the two keyboards plucking the strings at different points along their lengths. Plucking a string in the middle gives a rich, round **tone,** while a string plucked nearer the end has a hard, bright tone. Interesting effects could be obtained by playing the two keyboards at once, or by "echoing" notes on one keyboard with notes on the other. Extra sets of strings could be "switched on" by moving levers called **stops** (named after organ stops). These levers could be operated by hand or with pedals. Harpsichords continued to be made after the invention of the piano, so it seems reasonable to think that harpsichord makers felt the need to keep improving in order to compete with this new instrument.

The spinet is like a smaller version of the harpsichord and is therefore more suitable for home use than the harpsichord itself.

Playing techniques

Harpsichord players themselves also thought of ways of overcoming the shortcomings of the instrument, often by using creative playing techniques that would deceive the listeners' ears. These included playing quickly or slowly to give the impression that the music was louder or quieter and using trills (two **adjacent** notes played very quickly one after the other) to imply a single sustained note.

The Clavichord

The clavichord is a very old instrument. It may have been developed from a very early, simple instrument called the **monochord,** that consisted of a single string, a **soundbox,** and a movable **bridge.** Regardless, the clavichord had a very interesting history.

Internal workings

The keys of a clavichord are fastened in the middle, so that when a key is pressed, the opposite end rises up like a seesaw. The end of the key has a blunt metal blade on it, called a **tangent.** Strings are stretched across the interior of the instrument so that each blade strikes a pair of strings (tuned to the same note) when the key is pressed. When the key is released, the tangent moves away from the strings. On simpler types of clavichords, there are fewer strings, and each tangent strikes them in a different place. This gives a range of notes from each single string.

Some styles of clavichords are fairly large.

Clavichords at home

The sound of the clavichord is quiet and delicate. For this reason, it was mainly used in the home, until the piano and harpsichord replaced it as the usual home keyboard instruments in the eighteenth century. In that sense, it was the ancestor of today's electronic home keyboard. However, clavichords are still made today. While they are mainly used by keyboard specialists to play period music, one manufacturer has promoted the clavichord as the ideal nonelectronic instrument for music students, because the smallest types are very light and portable, and they also won't disturb the neighbors!

A versatile instrument

Unlike the harpsichord, the clavichord was valued for the subtle ways in which its sound could be changed. Its simple action meant that the loudness of the sound could be controlled by striking the keys harder. Pressing the keys down could make the notes higher, by stretching the strings with the tangent. Wobbling a key from side to side created a subtle **vibrato** effect, similar to that used by violinists.

Smaller tabletop clavichords were popular for use in the home in the seventeenth and eighteenth centuries.

Organ practice

One type of clavichord made in the mid-eighteenth century had a set of pedals laid out like a second keyboard and attached to strong vertical wires. When the pedals were pressed, the wires would operate a second mechanism underneath the main one. This type required a hands-and-feet technique like that used on a pipe organ, so some organists used it at home as a practice instrument.

The Pipe Organ

A type of pipe organ seems to have been the very first keyboard instrument of all. Over the centuries, the instrument has developed significantly. However, the basic principle of its operation has remained constant. Air is pumped through a set of pipes, with the sound of the instrument being changed by diverting the air into different pipes using a set of **valves** called **stops.** Pipe organs were originally powered by hand- or foot-operated **bellows,** but modern instruments have electric pumps instead.

Church organs

The pipe organ is mainly associated with churches, and it had become popular for church music by the fifteenth century. Because of their enormous size, these instruments were often built into the buildings they were housed in, and design preferences varied from region to region. For example, the Rhineland area of what is now Germany boasted some of the most technically advanced organs, some with two or three separate keyboards (known as **manuals**). Italian and French organs were simpler, usually with a single manual and a small range of stops. English organ builders were particularly interested in creating a wider variety of sounds for the instrument, and experimented with **reed stops** that sent the air into pipes that also contained **reeds.** English organ design suffered a setback in the seventeenth century—the church decided that the loud noise was inappropriate for pious worship, and many church organs were destroyed.

This is an early Baroque pipe organ at Guimiliau church in Germany.

Theater organs

Organs were first installed in theaters and cinema buildings in the early twentieth century. They were usually used to provide musical accompaniment for silent films and shows and for playing musical interludes between onstage performances. They were also installed in other places of entertainment, such as ice rinks. The working principles of these

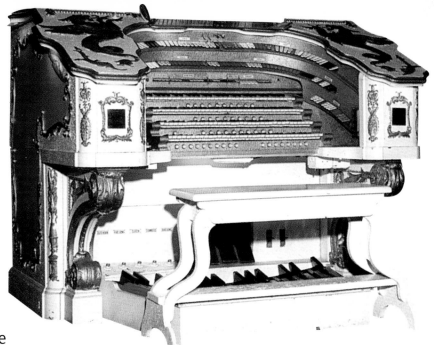

Many highly decorative theater organs have been preserved by enthusiasts and are still played in performances today.

instruments were the same as for other pipe organs, but they differed in the way they were "voiced," or how the pipes sounded. Because they were associated with recreation, they would often have a warm, jolly **tone.** The cheery sound of the theater organ often included sound effects made by **percussion** instruments that were built into the organ's mechanism.

Concert organs

Because the pipe organ is capable of producing a very powerful, varied, and expressive sound, instruments were also built into concert halls. Concert hall instruments were similar to church organs in design and were often very large, in order to accommodate the wide variety of music played on them. Organists could showcase their skills in **solo** organ recitals or could play concertos that were accompanied by a full orchestra. Other more complex works, including masses and **oratorios,** often required an organ, an orchestra, a choir, and even vocal soloists. The largest pipe organ in the world is a concert hall organ in the Atlantic City Convention Hall in Atlantic City, New Jersey. It has 33,112 pipes; 1,255 stops; and a total of seven manuals.

Reed Organs

Unlike most keyboard instruments, **reed** organs produce sounds by forcing air over metal reeds that then vibrate. Because of this unique way of producing sounds, reed organs are related to two other instrument families that are played in quite different ways. One is the group of wind instruments that includes the Chinese *sheng*, as well as the **Western** harmonium and melodica that were developed from it. The other is the group of **bellows**-operated metal reed instruments that include the accordion, melodeon, and concertina. Of these, the free-**bass** accordion is perhaps the closest relative to the reed organ. It gets its name from its design, with a keyboard at each end that allows the player a free choice of bass notes, instead of using the fixed **chords** produced by buttons. It could be thought of as a reed organ split in half and played sideways.

The compact Western harmoniums were often used overseas by Christian missionaries to accompany hymns.

The Western harmonium

Because some models are designed to look like pipe organs (often to the extent of having false pipes attached), the Western harmonium is often thought of as being many centuries old. In fact, it was **patented** in Paris by an instrument designer named Alexandre Debain as recently as 1848. One of the main functions of the harmonium—a name that eventually became used for reed organs in general—was as a substitute for the pipe organ. While early pipe organs could be small, by the mid-nineteenth century, most organs were larger and were permanently installed in buildings. The harmonium was much lighter and smaller, and it could be transported fairly easily. This meant that harmoniums could be supplied to small churches in rural areas where pipe organs were not practical.

The electric harmonium

Before relatively cheap electronic keyboards were available, a simple form of electric harmonium for home use was offered for sale in stores. Known as the electric chord organ, it had an air pump operated by electricity (or sometimes batteries), a set of chord buttons like an accordion, and a keyboard.

The harmonium is often used at Indian celebrations and festivals.

The harmonium in India

The harmonium is used extensively in Indian music. The instrument usually used is a small type that may be rested directly on the floor or on a suitable surface or carried by the player with a strap. The keyboard is laid out like a Western keyboard and is played with one hand, while the player uses the other hand to pump a small set of bellows at the back of the instrument. Because the instrument is small, the air has only a short distance to travel between the bellows and the reeds. This design, combined with the fact that the action of the bellows is very direct and can be controlled by the player, gives the Indian harmonium a lively, agile sound.

Electromechanical and Early Electronic Keyboards

Experiments in producing musical sound electronically began at the end of the nineteenth century. Before long, many inventors were producing designs that added new dimensions to the music of the time. It was easy to adapt the workings of traditional keyboards so that the keys would function as a set of switches—this meant that the link between electronics and keyboard instruments was established quickly.

The Ondes Martenot

The "Ondes" was **patented** in 1922 by the French inventor Maurice Martenot. It works by using electronic **oscillators** that produce very pure musical **tones.** The player controls these oscillators both with the instrument's five-**octave** keyboard and by sliding a finger along a wire set below the keyboard. This design allowed the instrument to produce piping notes that sounded like birdsongs, as well as swooping **glissandi,** that sound quite unique, even in comparison with modern **digital** instruments. Because the instrument has such a distinctive tone, it is still being made and played today.

The Ondes Martenot is perhaps the best example of an early electronic keyboard still in regular use.

The electronic organ

The electronic organ was the forerunner of the enormous variety of electronic keyboard instruments in use today. However, one of the most important and well-known versions, invented in 1935 by American Laurens Hammond, was actually an **electromechanical** instrument. It used motorized disks, called **tonewheels,** that spun in a **magnetic** field to produce an **electric current.** This design was later adapted to produce musical notes

The Hammond organ has an instantly recognizable sound.

that could be modified by **sliders** (called "drawbars") that changed the tone. Hammond originally intended the instrument to be used as a substitute for the pipe organ, both in religious settings and at home. However, its sounds, that had a distinctive "warble" (known as **vibrato**) and that could be varied from smooth and mellow to sharp and penetrating proved to be a great success with rock and jazz musicians. Unlike modern digital instruments, the Hammond organ has a slightly inconsistent sound, giving it a feel more like that of an **acoustic** instrument. For this reason, classic Hammonds are still sought after by musicians today. Several other manufacturers also made electronic organs of various types.

The electric piano and Clavinet

The original electric piano was also an electromechanical instrument. It was invented by an American named Harold Rhodes in the late 1940s. Rhodes's design used a keyboard that caused **hammers** to strike small metal plates inside the instrument. The sound was then **amplified** electronically. Rhodes had developed his invention from the simple, homemade instruments that he had been using to provide **occupational therapy** for wounded American airmen. His instrument had a smooth, bell-like sound that is still sought after by rock and jazz musicians today. Other manufacturers also made electric pianos, including one unusual model called the **Clavinet**—a type of large, amplified clavichord with a cutting, "funky" sound.

Early Synthesizers

All instruments could be said to be "synthesizers" in the sense that they create sounds that do not exist in the natural world. However, all conventional instruments do have their own natural sounds, and musicians and philosophers had wondered for centuries if it would ever be possible to assemble any sound from its most basic **components.** The story of the development of the synthesizer, an instrument that produces sounds purely electronically, is essentially the story of this idea being put into action. The earliest synthesizers were quite distinct from **electromechanical** instruments such as the Hammond organ and the electric piano, that produced only a very specific type of sound.

The RCA Synthesizer had a "typewriter" keyboard.

The first synthesizer

The earliest experiments with sounds other than those produced by conventional instruments involved the use of sound recordings. Various techniques were used, such as recording the sounds of "noninstruments" like pots and pans, and then cutting and rejoining the recording tape so that the sounds changed unexpectedly. However, this method was both time-consuming and artificial in that the results could exist only as a final recording and not as a live performance. This situation began to change with the 1955 invention of the first electronic synthesizer, the RCA Electronic Music Synthesizer, at the Sarnoff Research Center in New Jersey. However, this early synthesizer was a large, bulky instrument that had to be programmed using a roll of punched paper—so again, live performance was not possible. It did have a "keyboard," although it looked more like a typewriter and was used for punching holes in the paper roll.

Robert Moog's innovations

It was not until 1964 that synthesizers became widely available. The most important development was the invention of a system called "voltage control" by synthesizer pioneer Robert Moog. The type of electronic **synthesis** commonly used at the time involved electronic sound-producing circuits called **oscillators,** but these had to be individually tuned to the note chosen by the user. Moog invented a method of controlling the **pitch** of an oscillator using electrical power and standardized the amount of power needed at one volt per **octave.** This meant that a given amount of power would produce the chosen note just by switching the power on. This system was ideally suited to keyboard control, since a row of switches in the layout of a keyboard was easy to make. It was only at this point that the synthesizer began to look like a keyboard instrument. Even then, synthesizers without keyboards continued to be produced.

Portable synthesizers

After establishing the basic design of the keyboard-controlled synthesizer, Moog worked on refining the practical aspects of what was still a rather bulky instrument. This work resulted in the launch of the Mini-Moog in 1970. It was a fully portable, self-contained synthesizer controlled by a built-in keyboard. Its design allowed it to be used onstage by rock bands, alongside other keyboards such as the electronic organ and electric piano.

The Mini-Moog was the first portable keyboard synthesizer.

Polyphonic Synthesizers, Samplers, and Workstations

Since the first commercially available keyboard synthesizers were produced in the 1960s, the development of **polyphonic** synthesizers, **samplers,** and workstations have been the most significant advances in electronic keyboard technology. Each innovation added a new dimension to the playing of electronic keyboards.

The need for polyphonic synthesis

After Robert Moog had perfected the portable keyboard synthesizer, the next problem to be solved was that of polyphony, or the ability of a synthesizer to play more than one note at a time. Unlike conventional keyboard instruments, both the Mini-Moog and other similar instruments were limited to playing single notes. Even the earlier electronic organ and electric piano did not have this shortcoming. This problem had two immediate effects on the instruments' use. First, rock keyboard players usually added a synthesizer to their usual organ or piano setup rather than using synthesizers on their own. Second, synthesizer players had to develop various techniques to disguise the **monophonic** (single-note) nature of their instruments. These included playing very fast **arpeggios** that gave the impression of **chords** and playing two instruments simultaneously.

The first "polysynths"

With the invention of the microchip, it became possible to make much smaller electronic circuits. This allowed Robert Moog's company to produce the first satisfactory polyphonic synthesizer, the PolyMoog, in 1978. Effectively, the instrument had the most important circuits duplicated on a separate chip for each key. However, since each key had to be programmed individually, the range of sounds it produced was limited. Shortly afterward, another company launched a synthesizer called the Prophet 5 that solved this problem by "memorizing" control settings for different sounds.

Digital technology now allows all the necessary information to produce polyphonic sound to be stored in the instrument as computer data.

Keyboard samplers

Keyboard instruments that can play back prerecorded sounds date back to a 1960s instrument called the Mellotron, that used prerecorded tape. However, in 1979, an instrument was launched that could also "sample" any sound by making a digital recording of it and converting it into a musical **scale.** The Fairlight CMI (Computer Musical Instrument) was manufactured until 1988, but it was bulky and very expensive (the final version cost up to $175,000). Sampling soon became a common feature of much smaller, cheaper keyboards, either as an active process or as a means of supplying the instrument with preloaded sounds.

The music workstation

Together with polyphony and sampling, the invention of **sequencing**—the ability of an instrument to memorize a series of notes and replay them as required—made it possible for the keyboard player to create and record entire **compositions** with many parts on a single instrument. Composers who write and record music this way often use a workstation, which usually features a computer with programs that allow the composer to sequence the different parts of a composition. The workstation may also have a **controller keyboard** that is patched directly into the computer.

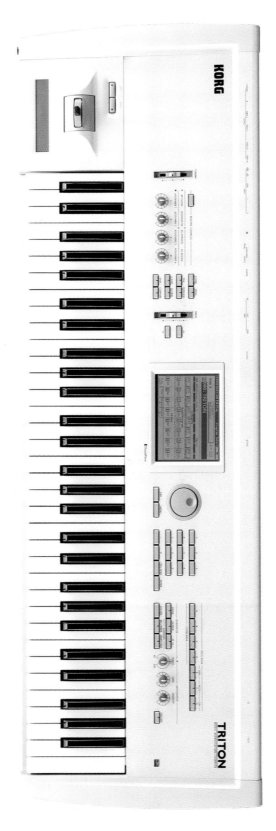

This cheap home keyboard has a built-in sequencer.

Computers, Keyboards, and Music

The technology used in computers and keyboard instruments allows them to "talk" to each other in many ways.

Early experiments

Computers were first used to make music without necessarily involving keyboards. Early computer-generated music often used computers to "translate" mathematical data into sound information—one example is Charles Dodge's 1970 **composition,** "Earth's **Magnetic** Field." Computers could also "write" compositions for conventional instruments based on random numbers or on a mathematical system. However, the development in the 1980s of a computer language called **MIDI** (Musical Instrument Digital Interface) allowed keyboards and computers to communicate and work together.

Computers like this one can be accessed from a keyboard using a MIDI connection.

What MIDI does

MIDI allows electronic musical instruments to transmit and receive musical information in the form of computer data. This information can tell what notes to play, in what order, at what **tempo,** at what volume, how long the notes should be, and so on. This kind of connection can allow one electronic keyboard to play the sounds of another, or a keyboard that may have no built-in sounds to play the sounds of any number of keyboardless "sound modules." These instruments contain the means to produce sounds, but have no built-in way of playing them. This arrangement gives the player a massive choice of sounds, all of which can be controlled from one keyboard if required. MIDI also allows music to be stored as data **sequences,** that can then be played back, edited, and so on, using either a computer or a smaller unit known as a sequencer.

MIDI, keyboards, and computers

Even most ordinary home PCs now have some capability for making music. With a MIDI connection to a computer, a user can:

- use a keyboard to play the sounds in the PC's sound card (the circuit supplied with most PCs for producing sound),
- record a musical performance using a keyboard and edit it using one of the many software packages available for this purpose, and
- store the performance on a disk and replay it elsewhere.

Computers and sound editing

The computer can help the electronic keyboard player in many other ways. One example is by the use of a type of software called a patch editor. Early synthesizers such as the Mini-Moog were covered in knobs and switches for changing the sound. Later synthesizers had more sophisticated sounds, but they often had to be programmed by using small, multifunction buttons and layers of tiny menus displayed on a small LCD screen on the instrument. Patch editor software "unfolds" all this information onto a computer screen. The user can then see all the ways in which the sound can be changed, make adjustments with mouse clicks, and send the results to the keyboard via MIDI. This editing technology has become increasingly important with the increase in the complexity of electronic keyboard instruments.

This sequencer can be programmed with keyboardlike buttons and can store musical phrases.

Innovative Keyboards

Keyboard instruments have had a central role in **Western** music for centuries. Today, most forms of music from many times and places are being preserved, performed,

The Yamaha DJX keyboard is "DJ-friendly."

and recorded somewhere in the world, meaning that there is a continued demand for appropriate keyboard instruments for each style. It is unlikely, therefore, that any individual type of keyboard instrument is going to disappear. Moreover, manufacturers are spending a great deal of time and effort in keeping up with demand.

Classical music

The piano, organ, harpsichord, and other keyboard instruments generally associated with classical music remain in huge demand. Some instruments, like the piano, generate more interest than others, like the clavichord. While the piano is popular and will be made in specialized factories for the foreseeable future, other instruments are generally handmade by individual craftspeople or assembled from kits.

Occasionally, **digital** technology is used in classical performance. One example is when an amateur orchestra uses an electronic keyboard (playing an appropriate sound) as a substitute for a harpsichord, because the cost of hiring and tuning a real harpsichord can be very expensive. However, **acoustic** keyboard instruments will never be completely replaced by electronic substitutes, because electronic instruments need to be played through an **amplifier** and loudspeakers. Because their sound is produced so differently, these instruments can never exactly reproduce the sounds of the instruments they imitate.

Keyboards in demand

With so many styles of music being created (and recreated) in this field, demand for all types of keyboard instruments will probably remain strong, and may even increase. The following are a few examples:

- **Hybrid** instruments are fairly recent innovations. One example, the Yamaha DJX keyboard, combines a keyboard design with the digital equivalent of "scratch mixing" facilities used by DJs.

- "Retro" keyboards (such as the Hammond organ),manufactured in the early days of electronic keyboards are in great demand. There will probably be further developments in re-creating their sounds on modern keyboards.

- "Soft-synth" keyboards are a particularly interesting group of instruments. In an attempt to make keyboard sounds available at the lowest possible cost, some companies are producing "keyboard instruments" that exist only as software. When loaded into a computer, the software simulates the sounds of the desired instrument and displays an interactive image of it on the screen, complete with an image of the keyboard layout. This image can then be operated via a **sequencer** or **controller keyboard** or "played" on screen by clicking the "keys" using a mouse.

This "soft" keyboard on a computer screen comes complete with virtual coffee stains.

Glossary

acoustic referring to sound; also can describe an unamplified instrument

adjacent next to each other

aerophone instrument that produces sound by using wind

amplify to make louder

arpeggio group of notes that are sounded individually in sequence

bass lowest range of notes in general use

bellows folded boxlike pouch, often made of leather, used to pump air into instruments such as reed and pipe organs

bowed played with a bow (a stick with a length of hair attached)

bridge sharp vertical edge on a stringed instrument, over which the strings are stretched

chord group of notes sounded simultaneously

chordophone instrument that produces sound using vibrating strings

Clavinet kind of electromechanical instrument that works like a clavichord but has its sound amplified electronically

component part of something

composition piece of written music

controller keyboard electronic keyboard that produces no sound itself, but that is used to access sounds stored in another electronic instrument or in a computer

damper device that mutes or muffles the sound of an instrument

digital using a "language" of ones and zeros

dynamics loudness or softness of a sound

electric current passage of electricity through conductive material

electromechanical using a mixture of electrical and mechanical means to make sounds

glissando sound made by "sliding" from one note to another

hammer part of the keyboard mechanism that hits the strings

hurdy-gurdy stringed instrument operated by a handle that rubs a rosin-covered wheel against the strings

hybrid cross between two types of things

idiophone percussion instrument that produces sound directly, such as a gong or woodblock

magnetic involving magnets or magnetism

manual keyboard on an organ or harpsichord; means "played by hand"

membranophone instrument, such as a drum, that makes a sound with a vibrating membrane

MIDI stands for Musical Instrument Digital Interface; a type of computer language that allows some electronic instruments to exchange data with computers and with each other

monochord early instrument with a single string

monophonic able to produce only one note at a time

musicologist person who studies aspects of music other than performance or composition, such as its history and cultural role

notation system of writing down music

occupational therapy constructive tasks given to victims of illness or injury to aid in their rehabilitation

octave eight tones that make up a musical scale

oratorio dramatic, usually religious musical work for orchestra and voices

oscillator electronic circuit that produces an output that can be heard as a musical note

patented licensed by the government as the inventor's original design

percussion type of instruments played by striking (or, in a few cases, friction)

pick small, flat object used to pluck the strings of certain stringed instruments

pickup electronic device attached to an instrument that allows it to be amplified electronically

pitch highness or lowness of a note

polyphony having two or more sounds at once

reed strip of cane that vibrates when air is blown across it

reed stop stop on an organ that allows air to pass through pipes that contain reeds

sample short digital sound recording stored in the memory of a computer or electronic instrument

scale arrangement of notes in ascending or descending order of pitch

sequence specific order of things (such as musical notes); or to place things in order

shutter door that closes off a space

slider device on early organs that was slid in and out to divert air into specific pipes

solo section or piece of music featuring a single performer with a group; one person performing alone is called a soloist

soundbox hollow object or structure used to amplify the sound of an instrument

stop hand-operated valve on a reed or pipe organ that allows air into particular pipes; also used for a mechanical control on a harpsichord

sustain to keep something, like a note, going for a long time

synthesis making or constructing something out of individual parts

tangent small metal hammer that strikes the strings of a clavichord

tempo speed at which a piece of music is played

tone quality of a sound

tonewheel metal disk used in a "classic" electronic organ—it produces sound by spinning in a magnetic field

valve device that regulates the flow of something, such as air in a wind instrument or electric current in an electronic organ

vibrato effect produced by continuous variation in the pitch of a note

West/ern North America and the countries of Europe; of or relating to North America and the countries of Europe

zither box-shaped instrument with strings that are plucked or strummed

Further Reading

Barber, Nicola (ed.). *The Kingfisher Young People's Book of Music*. New York: Larousse Kingfisher Chambers, 1999.

Dearling, Robert. *Keyboard Instruments & Ensembles: Encyclopedia of Musical Instruments*. Broomall, Penn.: Chelsea House Publishers, 2000.

Rowe, Julian. *Music*. Chicago: Heinemann Library, 1998.

Index